100 Ways to Say No Without Guilt.

-MINI BOOK-

100 Ways to Say No Without Guilt.

MINI BOOK-

A powerful tool to saying "NO" and rejecting people, situations and circumstances.

By Isaac Ajala

Copyright

Copyright © 2025 Isaac Ajala
All rights reserved.

No part of this publication may be reproduced, distributed, or transmitted in any form or by any means, including photocopying, recording, or other electronic or mechanical methods, without the prior written permission of the publisher, except in the case of brief quotations embodied in critical reviews or certain other non-commercial uses permitted by copyright law.

For permission requests, write to the publisher at: *majenquires@gmail.com*

This book is a work of nonfiction. The exercises and guidance herein are designed for personal development and educational purposes only. The author does not guarantee results and assumes no responsibility for individual outcomes. Consult a professional if you require mental health or medical support.

First Edition: June 2025

Table of Contents

Phrase 1. 10

Phrase 2. 12

Phrase 3. 14

Phrase 4. 16

Phrase 5. 18

Phrase 6. 20

Phrase 7. 22

Phrase 8. 24

Phrase 9. 26

Phrase 10. 28

Phrase 11. 30

Phrase 12. 32

Phrase 13. 34

Phrase 14. 36

Phrase 15. 38

Phrase 16. 40

Phrase 17. 42

Phrase 18. 44

Phrase 19. 46

Phrase 20. 48

Phrase 21. 50

Phrase 22. 52

Phrase 23. 54

Phrase 24. 56

Phrase 25. 58

Phrase 26	60
Phrase 27	62
Phrase 28	64
Phrase 29	66
Phrase 30	68
Phrase 31	70
Phrase 32	72
Phrase 33	74
Phrase 34	76
Phrase 35	78
Phrase 36	80
Phrase 37	82
Phrase 38	84
Phrase 39	86
Phrase 40	88
Phrase 41	90
Phrase 42	92
Phrase 43	94
Phrase 44	96
Phrase 45	98
Phrase 46	100
Phrase 47	102
Phrase 48	104
Phrase 49	106
Phrase 50	108
Phrase 51	110
Phrase 52	112
Phrase 53	114

Phrase 54.	116
Phrase 55.	118
Phrase 56.	120
Phrase 57.	122
Phrase 58.	124
Phrase 59.	126
Phrase 60.	128
Phrase 61.	130
Phrase 62.	132
Phrase 63.	134
Phrase 64.	136
Phrase 65.	138
Phrase 66.	140
Phrase 67.	142
Phrase 68.	144
Phrase 70.	148
Phrase 71.	150
Phrase 72.	152
Phrase 73.	154
Phrase 74.	156
Phrase 75.	158
Phrase 76.	160
Phrase 77.	162
Phrase 78.	164
Phrase 80.	168
Phrase 81.	170
Phrase 82.	172
Phrase 83.	174

Phrase 84	176
Phrase 85	178
Phrase 86	180
Phrase 87	182
Phrase 88	184
Phrase 89	186
Phrase 90	188
Phrase 91	190
Phrase 92	192
Phrase 93	194
Phrase 94	196
Phrase 95	198
Phrase 96	200
Phrase 97	202
Phrase 98	204
Phrase 99	206
Phrase 100	208
Closing Page	210
Certificate of Completion	211
Final Words	212

How To Use This Book:

You're not rude. You're not selfish. You're just allowed to say no.

This book is your everyday permission slip to protect your time, energy, and peace — without guilt, apology, or second-guessing.

Inside, you'll find **100 powerful ways to say "No"** that are clear, respectful, and effective. Each phrase comes with a breakdown of:

- Why it works
- When to use it
- How to say it with confidence

Some are gentle. Others are direct. All of them are designed to help you **reject requests** that don't serve you — while still honouring your relationships, values, and self-respect.

INSTRUCTIONS:

1. Read a few phrases a day — like flashcards for personal boundaries.
2. Practice out loud — the more you rehearse, the easier it gets.
3. Keep it on you — use it like a toolkit when you need real-time support.
4. Highlight your favourites — mark the ones that speak to your voice.
5. Revisit often — especially after moments when you gave in but wish you hadn't.

Saying no is not a weakness.

It's the strongest form of self-respect.

Let's rebuild your boundaries — one powerful "No" at a time.

Phrase 1.

"Thanks for thinking of me, but I'll have to pass this time."

This phrase is polite, appreciative, and firm. It acknowledges the request while clearly opting out — without inviting negotiation. The use of "this time" softens the rejection but still sets a boundary.

When to use it:

- When a friend invites you to an event you're not interested in.

- When a coworker asks you to stay late and cover a shift.

- When someone asks you to join a group project, committee, or social cause that isn't aligned with your priorities.

Example:

Your colleague asks, "Hey, want to help organize the company party?" You respond:

"Thanks for thinking of me, but I'll have to pass this time."

It leaves no room for guilt — and no door wide open for pushback.

Phrase 2.

"That's not something I can commit to right now."

This phrase is honest, direct, and sets a boundary without over-explaining. It gently reinforces that your time and energy are limited — and you're choosing where they go. The beauty is in its **calm confidence** — it's not personal, just a matter of current capacity.

When to use it:

- When a friend asks you to help move but you're already stretched thin
- When someone at work wants you to take on "just one more task"
- When a family member volunteers you for something without asking

Example:

Your sister says, "Can you plan the family reunion this year?"

You respond:

"That's not something I can commit to right now."

No excuses, no guilt, no wiggle room. Just clarity.

Phrase 3.
"I'm choosing to focus on other priorities right now."

This phrase puts you in control. You're not rejecting the person — you're **choosing yourself**. The word "choosing" shows intentionality, and "priorities" signals maturity and clarity. It doesn't invite guilt — it models self-respect.

When to use it:

- When someone tries to pull you into drama or distraction
- When asked to commit to something that doesn't align with your goals
- When declining extra obligations that compete with your time

Example:
Your friend asks, "Want to start this side hustle with me?"
You reply:

"I'm choosing to focus on other priorities right now."

No need to justify which priorities — the phrase stands on its own.

Phrase 4.

"I appreciate the offer, but I'll have to say no."

This is the perfect blend of politeness and firmness. You acknowledge the other person's effort or invitation while still clearly drawing the line. It keeps the tone respectful but makes your decision unshakable.

When to use it:

- When you're offered an opportunity you're not interested in
- When someone asks you to join a group, club, or commitment you don't align with
- When someone flirts or offers something you're not comfortable accepting

Example:

A coworker says, "Want to join us for drinks after work?"

You say:

"I appreciate the offer, but I'll have to say no."

You honour them — without compromising yourself.

Phrase 5.

"That doesn't work for me."

It's short, clear, and **non-negotiable**. It doesn't leave space for argument or guilt. You're not explaining yourself — you're stating a boundary. This phrase is ideal when you want to keep it **simple and strong**.

When to use it:

- When declining a request that oversteps your personal time
- When you're pressured to agree to something that makes you uncomfortable
- When someone tries to change plans or expectations last minute

Example:

Your boss says, "Can you stay late every day this week?"

You respond:

"That doesn't work for me."

No drama. No justification. Just a clear limit.

Phrase 6.

"I need to say no — thank you for understanding."

This phrase is gentle yet firm. By stating "I need to," you give yourself permission to protect your time or peace. Adding "thank you for understanding" assumes the best from the other person — which often encourages them to respect your boundary.

When to use it:

- When turning down a friend or loved one, and you want to soften the impact
- When setting a boundary with someone who usually pushes back
- When declining a request but still want to maintain the relationship

Example:

A friend says, "Can I crash at your place this weekend?"

You respond:

"I need to say no — thank you for understanding."

You hold the line, without sounding harsh.

Phrase 7.

"No, but I wish you the best with it."

This phrase sets a **clear boundary** while expressing goodwill. It's ideal for situations where you care about the other person but still want to say no. It also keeps the emotional tone warm and mature — you're declining, not disconnecting.

When to use it:

- When declining a friend's project, business, or opportunity
- When someone is selling or pitching something
- When you want to maintain kindness without sacrificing your own path

Example:

Someone says, "Would you like to invest in my startup idea?"

You say:

"No, but I wish you the best with it."

It ends the conversation respectfully — and without guilt.

Phrase 8.

"I'm not available for that."

This is short, firm, and confident — it **closes the door without sounding rude**. You're not explaining why or justifying yourself. You're simply declaring your unavailability, which commands respect.

When to use it:

- When someone keeps asking you for Favors
- When a friend expects your time, but you need rest
- When you're invited to something you don't want to attend

Example:
A friend texts, "Can you help me move this weekend?"
You reply:

"I'm not available for that."

Direct. Clean. Zero guilt.

Phrase 9.

"I'm focusing on myself right now, so I'll have to decline."

This phrase sends a strong message of **self-respect**. It frames your "no" as part of a bigger commitment to your well-being, not as rejection of the other person. It empowers you — and often inspires quiet respect.

When to use it:

- When you're invited out but need time alone
- When someone asks for emotional labour you can't offer
- When saying yes would sacrifice your peace or healing

Example:

A friend says, "Want to come out and blow off steam tonight?"

You say:

"I'm focusing on myself right now, so I'll have to decline."

You protect your space without apology — and model what self-prioritizing looks like.

Phrase 10.

"That's not aligned with where I'm heading right now."

This is a powerful, future-focused statement. It makes your "no" about **growth and direction**, not rejection. It shows you're living with intention — and anything that doesn't support your goals can be respectfully declined.

When to use it:

- When someone offers an opportunity that doesn't align with your vision
- When friends ask you to participate in habits or routines you've outgrown
- When you're invited into commitments that pull you off track

Example:

Someone says, "Want to start that side hustle again?"

You respond:

"That's not aligned with where I'm heading right now."

You're not just saying no — you're saying yes to your purpose.

Phrase 11.

"I'm honoured you asked, but I can't take that on."

This phrase shows **gratitude and humility**, while still being assertive. You're recognizing the compliment or trust in the request — but firmly declining it. It's a respectful "no" that keeps relationships strong without betraying your boundaries.

When to use it:

- When someone offers you a role, responsibility, or opportunity you don't want
- When a friend asks for help and you truly don't have capacity
- When you're flattered, but know it's not right for you

Example:

A team lead says, "We'd love for you to run this new initiative."

You reply:

"I'm honoured you asked, but I can't take that on."

It's graceful. It's clear. And it keeps your dignity — and theirs — intact.

Phrase 12.

"I don't have the capacity for that right now."

This phrase is honest, grounded, and impossible to argue with. It acknowledges your current mental, emotional, or physical limits without apology. You're not making excuses — you're stating reality. And **that's powerful**.

When to use it:

- When someone asks for your time and you're burned out
- When you're trying to avoid overcommitting
- When you've said "yes" too often and need to reclaim space

Example:

A friend says, "Can you help me brainstorm ideas tonight?"

You reply:

"I don't have the capacity for that right now."

It's honest. It's self-aware. And it gives you room to breathe.

Phrase 13.

"No, but thank you for thinking of me."

This phrase delivers a **clean and graceful no**. It's especially useful in personal or professional situations where you want to preserve warmth. It's polite, to the point, and leaves no ambiguity — which makes it ideal for boundary-setting with kindness.

When to use it:

- When turning down invitations, collaborations, or favours
- When declining offers that feel generous but misaligned
- When someone asks for your presence, but you simply can't commit

Example:

A colleague says, "Would you be open to mentoring me this quarter?"
You respond:

"No, but thank you for thinking of me."

You keep the door of goodwill open — without stepping through it.

Phrase 14.

"That's not something I'm available for."

This is a calm, composed refusal. It sounds professional and firm without being defensive. It shifts the focus away from *whether you want to* and makes it about your **availability** — which is harder to argue with.

When to use it:

- When someone asks for your time, presence, or resources
- When you're avoiding reactive "yeses" in the moment
- When you're being voluntold or pressured into saying yes

Example:

A family member says, "Can you take care of this for me today?"

You say:

"That's not something I'm available for."

It creates emotional distance while preserving respect.

Phrase 15.

"I'm learning to say no to protect my peace — this is one of those times."

This phrase is **vulnerable, honest, and empowering**. It invites empathy while reinforcing your boundary. You're not just saying no — you're saying yes to your growth, your healing, and your peace. It's especially powerful in emotionally close relationships.

When to use it:

- When you need to say no to loved ones who usually expect a yes
- When setting a new boundary with someone who's used to access
- When you want to express growth without guilt

Example:

A close friend says, "Can I vent to you tonight? I really need to talk."

You respond:

"I'm learning to say no to protect my peace — this is one of those times."

It's not rejection. It's respect — for yourself.

Phrase 16.

"That's not a priority for me right now."

This phrase is simple, direct, and puts the responsibility where it belongs — with your **priorities**, not the other person's expectations. It reminds others (and yourself) that your time is limited, and not everything deserves a yes.

When to use it:

- When asked to do something that distracts from your goals
- When someone expects your help, but it doesn't serve your current path
- When you feel pressured to take on extra responsibilities

Example:
A coworker says, "Can you take the lead on this extra project?"
You say:

"That's not a priority for me right now."

Clear. Professional. Guilt-free.

Phrase 17.

"I won't be able to help with that."

This phrase is short, calm, and **unapologetically clear**. It removes negotiation from the table. You're not offering alternatives, excuses, or explanations — just a firm boundary delivered with grace.

When to use it:

- When someone asks for a favour that feels like a burden
- When you want to shut down repeat requests with consistency
- When you don't owe the person anything more than honesty

Example:

A neighbour says, "Can you watch my dog this weekend?"

You respond:

"I won't be able to help with that."

Polite. Final. No guilt necessary.

Phrase 18.

"I've decided not to take anything else on right now."

This phrase communicates a **clear personal boundary** rooted in intentional choice. By saying "I've decided," you frame it as a confident, pre-made decision — which takes it out of the other person's control. It's not personal; it's a policy.

When to use it:

- When you're at capacity and don't want to explain details
- When someone tries to add to your plate casually
- When you're protecting your time or mental health

Example:

A teammate says, "Can you join this side project with us?"

You say:

"I've decided not to take anything else on right now."

It's a strong "no" — built on your right to choose.

Phrase 19.

"This isn't something I can say yes to."

This phrase is polite, thoughtful, and gently firm. It softens the blow without weakening your boundary. You're not just saying "no" — you're affirming your right to **choose what gets your yes**, and this isn't it.

When to use it:

- When turning down emotionally sensitive or high-pressure requests
- When someone expects your agreement by default
- When you're protecting yourself without burning bridges

Example:
A friend says, "Can you lend me money until next month?"
You respond:

"This isn't something I can say yes to."

You're calm, kind, and unshakably clear.

Phrase 20.

"That's not something I'm comfortable with."

This phrase sets a **boundary based on emotional truth**. It's firm but not confrontational — and the word *"comfortable"* makes it personal and non-negotiable. No one can argue with how you feel.

When to use it:

- When someone crosses a line or makes an inappropriate request
- When you're asked to do something that violates your values
- When your intuition says no, even if your logic wavers

Example:
A peer says, "Can you keep this between us, even if it's not right?"
You say:

"That's not something I'm comfortable with."

It puts your integrity and peace first — where they belong.

Phrase 21.

"That's not a responsibility I'm willing to take on."

This phrase makes it crystal clear that you've **considered the ask — and rejected it with intention.** It emphasizes your right to decide what responsibilities you accept and avoids emotional entanglement or guilt-tripping.

When to use it:

- When someone tries to delegate their work onto you
- When you're pressured to manage something outside your role
- When someone assumes you'll "step up" without asking first

Example:

A team member says, "Can you oversee this part of the project for me?"

You respond:

"That's not a responsibility I'm willing to take on."

You protect your boundaries — and your bandwidth.

Phrase 22.

"I'm saying no so I can say yes to what matters most."

This phrase reframes your refusal as a **positive, values-based decision**. You're not rejecting the person — you're honouring your deeper commitments. It gently teaches others that every "yes" costs something, and your time is sacred.

When to use it:

- When declining social invites that interrupt your priorities
- When choosing rest, recovery, or solitude over obligation
- When you're committing to a project, goal, or boundary

Example:
A friend says, "Are you free to help me reorganize this weekend?"
You respond:

"I'm saying no so I can say yes to what matters most."

It's self-respect in sentence form.

Phrase 23.

"I'm not the right person for that."

This phrase is clean, confident, and **shuts down obligation** without sounding dismissive. It subtly redirects the request without offering to help find someone else. You're asserting your boundaries **without guilt or over-explaining**.

When to use it:

- When someone asks you to do something outside your role or expertise
- When people assume you're the go-to for things you didn't agree to
- When you're expected to step in just because you usually do

Example:

A team member says, "Can you take care of the technical side of this?" You reply:

"I'm not the right person for that."

It communicates clarity — not coldness.

Phrase 24.

"I'm choosing to sit this one out."

This phrase is casual but intentional. It communicates that your **decision is active, not passive** — you're not being left out or unsure, you're *choosing* not to participate. It's perfect for maintaining good vibes while honouring your limits.

When to use it:

- When declining group activities, events, or obligations
- When you're tired of always being the "yes" person
- When you want to bow out without making it a big deal

Example:
Your friends say, "We're all signing up for this challenge — you in?"
You reply:

"I'm choosing to sit this one out."

You stay friendly — and firm.

Phrase 25.

"I've got too much on my plate to give that the attention it deserves."

This phrase shows **respect for the request**, while clearly stating that your current workload or energy doesn't allow you to do it justice. It's thoughtful, responsible, and establishes boundaries **without sounding dismissive or disinterested**.

When to use it:

- When asked to take on a task you know you'll have to rush
- When someone wants you to commit time you don't truly have
- When you care about doing things well — and know this one won't fit

Example:
Someone says, "Would you mind reviewing this whole document tonight?"
You respond:

"I've got too much on my plate to give that the attention it deserves."

It's not a brush-off — it's an honest standard of quality and self-awareness.

Phrase 26.

"I'm intentionally keeping my schedule light right now."

This phrase makes your "no" about **mindful living**, not avoidance. You're signalling that you're being selective with your time and energy — not because you're lazy, but because you're prioritizing what truly matters. It frames boundaries as wisdom.

When to use it:

- When turning down social plans during a reset period
- When someone expects your time out of routine, not respect
- When you want to honour your own need for margin and rest

Example:

A coworker asks, "Can we squeeze in a call after hours?"

You respond:

"I'm intentionally keeping my schedule light right now."

You're not overbooked — you're **consciously unavailable**.

Phrase 27.

"That's outside of what I'm able to offer right now."

This phrase is respectful and sets a **gentle but firm limit**. It signals that your resources — whether time, energy, or emotional bandwidth — are being managed intentionally. It's not a rejection of the person; it's a boundary around what you can give.

When to use it:

- When someone asks for a favour that requires more than you can give
- When you're expected to emotionally support others at your own expense
- When you're setting boundaries with recurring requests

Example:
A friend says, "Can you walk me through everything tonight?"
You reply:

"That's outside of what I'm able to offer right now."

It respects them — and protects you.

Phrase 28.

"I'm saying no because I value my time and energy."

This phrase is bold and unapologetic. It communicates that your "no" isn't about being difficult — it's about **knowing your worth**. It teaches people how to treat your boundaries by showing how much you honour them yourself.

When to use it:

- When others expect you to explain or justify your decisions
- When you're practicing assertiveness in a personal growth season
- When you want to reinforce your identity as someone with standards

Example:

Someone says, "Why not? It's just one little thing."

You respond:

"I'm saying no because I value my time and energy."

It's a boundary — and a reminder.

Phrase 29.

"I've learned that overcommitting drains me, so I have to pass."

This phrase is honest, reflective, and **rooted in self-awareness**. It shows that your "no" is a learned boundary — not a reactive decision. It subtly signals to others that you've paid the price before, and now you're protecting your peace.

When to use it:

- When someone invites you to "just one more thing"
- When you're tempted to say yes out of habit or guilt
- When you're drawing new boundaries people may not be used to

Example:

A friend says, "Come on, just commit to this one last favour."

You respond:

"I've learned that overcommitting drains me, so I have to pass."

It's wisdom. It's firm. And it honours your growth.

Phrase 30.

"I'm prioritizing rest right now, so I'll have to say no."

This phrase sends a clear message: **rest is a valid reason.** You don't owe anyone burnout. By naming rest as your priority, you model healthy boundaries and remind yourself — and others — that your well-being matters just as much as productivity.

When to use it:

- When you're asked to go out, take on more, or "push through"
- When you're recovering from stress, burnout, or emotional fatigue
- When you're learning to protect your energy without apology

Example:

A friend says, "Want to hang out late tonight after work?"

You respond:

"I'm prioritizing rest right now, so I'll have to say no."

It's calm. It's kind. And it's exactly what you need.

Phrase 31.

"That's not something I'm willing to take on."

This phrase expresses a firm boundary without inviting negotiation. It's not about ability or availability — it's about **choice and willingness**. It puts you in control and communicates that your "no" is final and self-respecting.

When to use it:

- When someone pressures you to say yes "just this once"
- When declining a role, responsibility, or favour you're done accepting
- When others assume you'll help just because you always have

Example:
A colleague says, "Can you handle the event logistics again this year?"
You respond:

"That's not something I'm willing to take on."

It's clear, confident, and keeps your peace protected.

Phrase 32.

"That's not a good fit for me."

This phrase is **short, neutral, and unarguable**. It avoids emotional entanglement or over-explaining and puts the decision back on personal alignment. It's especially effective in professional, networking, or social circles where diplomacy matters.

When to use it:

- When turning down a collaboration, job offer, or commitment
- When declining something that feels off, but hard to explain
- When you want to remain respectful without revealing too much

Example:

Someone says, "Would you be interested in joining our mastermind group?"

You respond:

"That's not a good fit for me."

Simple. Clean. Boundaries.

Phrase 33.

"I'm choosing to protect my time."

This phrase frames your "no" as a **deliberate act of self-respect**. It communicates maturity, mindfulness, and prioritization. You're not reacting — you're choosing. And protecting your time is never selfish; it's **essential**.

When to use it:

- When someone makes you feel guilty for saying no
- When you're declining plans, calls, or meetings that interrupt your flow
- When reclaiming time after overcommitting

Example:

A colleague says, "Can you hop on a quick call at 9 PM?"

You respond:

"I'm choosing to protect my time."

No guilt. No debate. Just clarity.

Phrase 34.

"That's not in alignment with my goals right now."

This phrase brings the focus back to your **personal mission and priorities**. It communicates that your "no" is not random — it's rooted in purpose. It also subtly reminds others that you're intentional about what you give your energy to.

When to use it:

- When turning down collaborations or social invites that don't match your vision
- When someone asks for your time on something that feels like a distraction
- When guarding your focus during a productive season

Example:

A friend says, "Want to join our group for a new side hustle idea?"

You respond:

"That's not in alignment with my goals right now."

Professional. Clear. Purpose-driven.

Phrase 35.

"I've got other priorities I'm focusing on right now."

This phrase gently asserts that you're not saying no out of disinterest — but out of **focus**. It communicates that your time and attention are already committed elsewhere, which makes your boundary feel both reasonable and mature.

When to use it:

- When declining an opportunity or favour without burning bridges
- When protecting your time from overcommitment
- When someone expects you to shift your focus for their request

Example:
A friend says, "Can you help me launch this new project with me?"
You say:

"I've got other priorities I'm focusing on right now."

It's honest. Respectful. And it keeps your time yours.

Phrase 36.

"I'm not in a place to commit to that."

This phrase signals emotional intelligence and self-awareness. It shows that you've assessed your **mental, emotional, or practical readiness**, and chosen to honour it. It's compassionate toward both yourself and the person asking — without crossing your boundary.

When to use it:

- When you're emotionally drained or in recovery
- When someone asks for your time, energy, or emotional labour
- When you're saying no to maintain balance and protect healing

Example:

A friend says, "Can you take this on for me while I deal with things?"

You reply:

"I'm not in a place to commit to that."

It's kind. It's true. And it gives you room to breathe.

Phrase 37.

"I'd rather not — but I appreciate you asking."

This phrase is casual yet assertive. It uses polite language ("I'd rather not") to communicate your **personal preference** without opening the door to negotiation. The added appreciation softens the message without weakening it.

When to use it:

- When someone offers you an opportunity you don't want
- When turning down invitations without drama
- When someone's making a request that feels low stakes but unwanted

Example:

A coworker says, "Want to join us for the office karaoke night?"

You respond:

"I'd rather not — but I appreciate you asking."

Friendly. Firm. Guilt-free.

Phrase 38.

"I've set a boundary around that."

This phrase is **bold, direct, and empowering**. It shows that your "no" is not a spur-of-the-moment reaction — it's a conscious boundary. It teaches others that your life has structure, and you're the one who builds it.

When to use it:

- When someone continues to push past your previous "no"
- When you're protecting yourself from toxic dynamics
- When you want to shut down negotiation completely

Example:

Someone says, "Why won't you help me again like before?"

You respond:

"I've set a boundary around that."

It's unapologetic — and it reinforces your right to protect your peace.

Phrase 39.

"I don't have space for that in my life right now."

This phrase is gentle, honest, and non-defensive. It shows your decision comes from intentional boundary-setting, not negativity. It allows you to say no while affirming your values.

When to use it:

- When you're protecting emotional or mental space.
- When someone repeatedly asks for your involvement.
- When setting boundaries without confrontation

Example:
A friend says, "Can we start hanging out every weekend again?"
You respond:
"I don't have space for that in my life right now."

You prioritise your space, purpose and focus without guilt.

Phrase 40.

"I'm not the best person to help with this."

This phrase removes pressure by redirecting the request away from you. It's not dismissive — it's strategic. It allows you to decline without creating conflict, maintaining respect and preserving your time.

When to use it:

- When you're protecting emotional or mental space.
- When someone repeatedly asks for your involvement.
- When setting boundaries without confrontation

Example:
A friend says, "Can we start hanging out every weekend again?"
You respond:
"I don't have space for that in my life right now."

You honour your time without guilt.

Phrase 41.

"This isn't a priority for me."

It's clear, confident, and grounded. It subtly reminds others that just because something is important to them doesn't mean it's important to you. This phrase protects your time and focus, without guilt or explanation.

When to use it:

- When someone keeps pushing their urgency onto you
- When setting boundaries with requests that don't align with your goals
- When you want to reclaim your calendar without feeling bad

Example:
A friend says, "Can you help me design my new blog?"
You respond:

"This isn't a priority for me."

Simple. Assertive. And unapologetically honest.

Phrase 42.

"I'm working on saying no more often — and this is one of those times."

This phrase is humble and empowering. It lets others know you're intentionally building new boundaries and gently closes the door with self-awareness. It shows growth without needing to explain yourself.

When to use it:

- When setting new boundaries with people who aren't used to hearing no
- When you want to own your growth journey without giving long explanations
- When turning down familiar requests or old patterns

Example:

A friend says, "Can I vent for the next hour?"

You reply:

"I'm working on saying no more often — and this is one of those times."

Growth doesn't need an apology.

Phrase 43.

"I need to honour my limits, so I'll have to say no."

This phrase is powerful because it comes from self-respect. You're not rejecting the person — you're respecting your boundaries. It conveys strength with kindness, making it clear you're prioritizing your well-being.

When to use it:

- When you're close to burnout or already overwhelmed
- When saying yes would mean sacrificing your own peace
- When you need language that reflects strength balanced with softness

Example:

A coworker says, "Can you take this on too?"

You respond:

"I need to honour my limits, so I'll have to say no."

It's permission to protect your energy.

Phrase 44.

"I'm committed to not overcommitting."

This phrase is punchy and clear. You've set a personal rule, and this phrase communicates that with strength. It shows proactive self-awareness, not passivity, making it clear you value balance and boundaries.

When to use it:

- When people expect you to always say yes
- When building new patterns of balance and rest
- When you want to create an internal boundary and external message

Example:
A friend says, "Want to jump into one more project?"
You respond:

"I'm committed to not overcommitting."

It's short, powerful, and anchored in growth.

Phrase 45.

"That's not something I'm open to."

This phrase communicates personal boundary with emotional maturity. It's firm without needing backstory. It shuts the door calmly and clearly, making your "no" non-negotiable without sounding harsh.

When to use it:

- When rejecting suggestions, advice, or emotional manipulation
- When someone offers something you've clearly declined before
- When you want your no to be final without sounding rude

Example:

Someone says, "Maybe you should just give them another chance."

You respond:

"That's not something I'm open to."

It's simple. Final. And strong.

Phrase 46.

"I'm practicing saying no to protect my peace."

This phrase is honest and transparent. It explains your no without seeking permission or approval. It shows maturity and self-awareness, helping others understand that you're choosing peace over obligation.

When to use it:

- When turning down emotional labour or draining conversations
- When declining invitations that would overwhelm you
- When honouring your energy during recovery or transition

Example:

A friend says, "Do you want to talk through this big issue right now?"
You respond:

"I'm practicing saying no to protect my peace."

You honour your limits — without guilt.

Phrase 47.

"No — not this time."

This is a soft but powerful refusal. It provides a sense of finality for now, without burning bridges. It's perfect for situations where you want to say no gently but firmly, leaving room for future possibilities.

When to use it:

- When declining something you might reconsider later
- When you want to avoid confrontation or drama
- When you want to set a boundary without closing the door completely

Example:

A family member says, "Can you take charge of the holiday plans again?" You respond:

"No — not this time."

It says enough — and no more.

Phrase 48.

"That's no longer something I say yes to."

This phrase acknowledges growth and change. It reinforces that you're no longer the person who accepts every request. It's a strong, clear boundary that honours your evolution.

When to use it:

- When breaking free from old habits or roles
- When people expect you to continue patterns you've outgrown
- When drawing a line between your past and your present self

Example:

An old friend says, "You always used to take care of this."

You reply:

"That's no longer something I say yes to."

You honour who you've become.

Phrase 49.

"I'm choosing to protect my energy."

This phrase is simple but powerful. It communicates that your refusal is about preserving your well-being, not rejecting others. It reinforces the importance of self-care as a valid reason to say no.

When to use it:

- When you're feeling drained and need to set limits
- When declining additional commitments to avoid burnout
- When others don't understand why you're saying no

Example:
A friend asks, "Can you come out tonight?"
You respond:

"I'm choosing to protect my energy."

It's honest, respectful, and firm.

Phrase 50.

"No."

It's fine to say no.

When to use it:

- When you don't want to say yes.
- When you feel pressured to say yes.
- When you feel it's right to say no.

Example:

A friend asks, "Do you want to drink with us tonight?

You respond:

"No."

It's fine to say no.

Phrase 51.

"I need to focus on my priorities right now."

This phrase clearly communicates that your time is valuable, and you are intentionally dedicating it to what matters most to you. It's a respectful but firm way to decline without making excuses.

When to use it:

- When someone asks you to take on something that conflicts with your goals
- When declining invitations that distract from your plans
- When you want to reinforce your commitment to your own success

Example:

A colleague asks, "Can you help me with this project?"

You respond:

"I need to focus on my priorities right now."

You set clear boundaries aligned with your values.

Phrase 52.

"I appreciate you thinking of me, but I have to decline."

This phrase is polite and respectful while maintaining firmness. It acknowledges the other person's thoughtfulness but clearly communicates your decision to say no without opening the door for negotiation.

When to use it:

- When declining invitations or offers politely
- When you want to maintain good relationships while setting boundaries
- When you want to avoid confrontation but need to be clear

Example:

A friend says, "Would you like to join us for dinner?"

You respond:

"I appreciate you thinking of me, but I have to decline."

It's courteous and direct.

Phrase 53.

"That doesn't fit with my current goals."

This phrase clearly communicates that your refusal is intentional and aligned with your personal growth. It sets a boundary without negativity and encourages others to respect your focus.

When to use it:

- When asked to participate in activities unrelated to your objectives
- When declining extra commitments that detract from your progress
- When setting clear priorities in your life

Example:
A colleague invites you to a networking event, but you're focused on writing your book.
You reply:

"That doesn't fit with my current goals."

It's honest, professional, and firm.

Phrase 54.

"I'm not able to take that on right now."

This phrase communicates your current capacity limits without negativity or excuses. It's respectful but firm, helping you protect your time and energy while maintaining good relationships.

When to use it:

- When asked for favours or tasks beyond your current availability
- When you want to decline without providing a detailed explanation
- When you want to assert boundaries calmly and clearly

Example:
A coworker asks, "Can you help with this report by tomorrow?"
You respond:

"I'm not able to take that on right now."

It's clear and guilt-free.

Phrase 55.

"I'm focusing on my well-being and need to say no."

This phrase is honest and heartfelt, emphasizing the importance of self-care. It lets others know your refusal comes from a place of taking care of yourself, which most people respect.

When to use it:

- When declining invitations that may harm your mental or physical health
- When setting boundaries around your personal time
- When you want to reinforce your commitment to self-care

Example:
A friend invites you to a late-night party, but you need rest.
You respond:

"I'm focusing on my well-being and need to say no."

It's sincere and clear.

Phrase 56.

"I'm unable to give that the attention it deserves."

This phrase communicates respect for both the request and your own standards. It shows that you don't want to commit half-heartedly and prefer to say no rather than deliver less than your best.

When to use it:

- When you're asked to take on tasks you can't fully commit to
- When you want to avoid overextending yourself
- When you want to express your intention to maintain quality

Example:

A colleague asks, "Can you handle this project?"

You respond:

"I'm unable to give that the attention it deserves."

It's honest and professional.

Phrase 57.

"I need to prioritize my current commitments."

This phrase clearly communicates that you're dedicated to what you've already agreed to and can't take on more. It's firm and respectful, making it easier for others to understand your boundaries.

When to use it:

- When asked to join new projects or tasks while you're busy
- When declining additional responsibilities at work or home
- When you want to reinforce commitment to your own goals

Example:

A colleague asks, "Can you help with this new initiative?"

You reply:

"I need to prioritize my current commitments."

It's straightforward and clear.

Phrase 58.

"I'm not comfortable taking that on right now."

This phrase communicates a clear personal boundary rooted in your comfort and readiness. It's honest and respectful, setting limits without inviting argument.

When to use it:

- When you're uncertain about a new responsibility
- When feeling overwhelmed by requests
- When you want to politely decline while preserving relationships

Example:
A friend asks, "Can you help organize the event next month?"
You respond:

"I'm not comfortable taking that on right now."

It's firm, clear, and considerate.

Phrase 59.

"I'm taking time to focus on what truly matters."

This phrase emphasizes intentionality and prioritization. It communicates that your "no" is part of a deliberate choice to invest your time and energy wisely.

When to use it:

- When declining distractions or low-priority tasks
- When setting boundaries around your goals and values
- When you want to highlight your commitment to meaningful pursuits

Example:
A friend invites you to an event you don't want to attend.
You say:

"I'm taking time to focus on what truly matters."

It's focused, intentional, and respectful.

Phrase 60.

"I need to protect my energy for other commitments."

This phrase clearly communicates that you are managing your resources thoughtfully. It's a respectful and firm way to decline while emphasizing self-care and responsibility.

When to use it:

- When you want to avoid burnout
- When declining additional tasks or favours
- When you want others to understand your limits

Example:

A colleague asks, "Can you take on this extra work this week?"

You respond:

"I need to protect my energy for other commitments."

It's honest, clear, and assertive.

Phrase 61.

"I'm choosing to say no to make room for my goals."

This phrase clearly links your refusal to your bigger vision, signalling intentionality and purpose. It helps others understand that your "no" is a positive, strategic choice.

When to use it:

- When declining distractions or non-essential requests
- When setting firm boundaries for your personal or professional growth
- When you want to reinforce your commitment to priorities

Example:

A friend invites you to join a hobby group that doesn't align with your goals. You say:

"I'm choosing to say no to make room for my goals."

It's confident, clear, and inspiring.

Phrase 62.

"I'm not available to help with that."

This phrase is simple, direct, and clear. It sets a boundary without needing to explain further, making it effective in both professional and personal situations.

When to use it:

- When you cannot offer assistance due to time or energy constraints
- When you want to decline without providing detailed reasons
- When you want to maintain professionalism while setting limits

Example:
A colleague asks, "Can you cover my shift next week?"
You reply:

"I'm not available to help with that."

It's firm and respectful.

Phrase 63.

"That's not something I'm comfortable committing to."

This phrase sets a clear, respectful boundary based on your comfort level. It conveys honesty without inviting argument, making it useful in many personal and professional contexts.

When to use it:

- When asked to join activities or projects that feel overwhelming
- When you want to decline without offending others
- When you prefer to maintain control over your commitments

Example:
A friend says, "Can you volunteer for the community event?"
You respond:

"That's not something I'm comfortable committing to."

It's straightforward and respectful.

Phrase 64.

"I'm focusing on what's best for me right now."

This phrase clearly communicates that your decision is rooted in self-care and prioritization. It lets others know your "no" comes from a place of self-respect, not rejection.

When to use it:

- When declining invitations or requests that do not support your well-being
- When setting boundaries with friends or family
- When reinforcing your commitment to personal growth

Example:

A colleague invites you to stay late for a meeting.

You reply:

"I'm focusing on what's best for me right now."

It's honest, clear, and confident.

Phrase 65.

"I'm choosing to say no to maintain my balance."

This phrase expresses a conscious decision to protect your mental and emotional equilibrium. It highlights the importance of balance in your life and explains your refusal as part of that priority.

When to use it:

- When overwhelmed by multiple demands
- When you need to safeguard your emotional health
- When declining tasks or commitments that would disrupt your routine

Example:

A friend asks, "Can you take on organizing the group trip?"
You respond:

"I'm choosing to say no to maintain my balance."

It's respectful, clear, and assertive.

Phrase 66.

"I need to focus my energy elsewhere."

This phrase clearly communicates that your priorities lie elsewhere, helping you say no without offending. It's straightforward and emphasizes intentionality.

When to use it:

- When you want to avoid overcommitting
- When you have limited time or resources
- When you want to decline politely but firmly

Example:
A colleague asks, "Can you help with this new client?"
You respond:

"I need to focus my energy elsewhere."

It's concise and respectful.

Phrase 67.

"I'm learning to protect my time and energy."

This phrase acknowledges that setting boundaries is a process. It communicates growth and self-awareness, encouraging others to respect your journey.

When to use it:

- When you're gradually establishing limits
- When others question your refusals
- When you want to emphasize personal development

Example:
A friend says, "Are you sure you don't want to help with this?"
You reply:

"I'm learning to protect my time and energy."

It's honest, humble, and firm.

Phrase 68.

"I'm saying no to create space for what matters most."

This phrase emphasizes intentionality behind your refusal. It shows that your "no" is a conscious choice to prioritize important aspects of your life.

When to use it:

- When turning down distractions or less important requests
- When managing time for personal or professional growth
- When you want to explain your boundaries with clarity

Example:

A friend invites you to a late-night party. You say:

"I'm saying no to create space for what matters most."

It's purposeful and empowering.

69.

"I'm not able to take on additional commitments right now."

This phrase is direct and clear, setting a firm boundary without inviting further discussion. It communicates your current limits respectfully.

When to use it:

- When feeling overwhelmed with existing responsibilities
- When someone asks for favours or help that you cannot accommodate
- When you want to keep boundaries firm but polite

Example:

A colleague says, "Can you join the new committee?"

You respond:

"I'm not able to take on additional commitments right now."

It's straightforward and respectful.

Phrase 70.

"Thank you for asking, but I need to decline."

This phrase is polite and appreciative, while firmly setting your boundary. It acknowledges the request and the thought behind it, making your refusal respectful and clear.

When to use it:

- When turning down invitations or offers graciously
- When you want to avoid conflict while saying no
- When maintaining good relationships is important

Example:
A friend says, "Would you like to join our book club?"
You respond:

"Thank you for asking, but I need to decline."

It's courteous and final.

Phrase 71.

"I'm focusing on my own needs right now."

This phrase clearly communicates your decision to prioritize yourself. It helps others understand that your no comes from self-care, not disregard.

When to use it:

- When declining social events or favours
- When setting personal boundaries with family or friends
- When reinforcing your commitment to well-being

Example:

A friend invites you to a weekend trip. You say:

"I'm focusing on my own needs right now."

It's honest, respectful, and firm.

Phrase 72.

"I'm not in a position to help right now."

This phrase is clear and straightforward, emphasizing your current unavailability without giving room for negotiation or guilt.

When to use it:

- When you want to decline a request politely
- When you are overwhelmed or busy
- When you want to assert boundaries calmly

Example:

A colleague asks, "Can you assist with this report?"

You respond:

"I'm not in a position to help right now."

It's firm, respectful, and to the point.

Phrase 73.

"I'm setting boundaries to protect my peace."

This phrase explains that your "no" is part of a deliberate effort to maintain your emotional and mental well-being. It encourages respect for your limits.

When to use it:

- When declining emotional labour or draining conversations
- When turning down additional commitments
- When others question your refusals

Example:

A friend says, "Can you talk about this issue now?"

You respond:

"I'm setting boundaries to protect my peace."

It's clear, assertive, and nurturing.

Phrase 74.

"I'm focusing on what's best for me."

This phrase asserts that your refusal is grounded in self-care and thoughtful decision-making. It sets a respectful boundary while emphasizing your priorities.

When to use it:

- When declining invitations or requests that don't support your well-being
- When protecting your time and energy
- When you want to be clear about your personal focus

Example:

A colleague asks, "Can you join the extra meeting?"

You respond:

"I'm focusing on what's best for me."

It's honest and empowering.

Phrase 75.

"I'm learning to prioritize myself."

This phrase highlights your growth and evolving boundaries. It communicates that saying no is part of your personal development, encouraging others to respect your journey.

When to use it:

- When setting new limits with friends or family
- When someone challenges your refusals
- When you want to express self-care as a priority

Example:
A friend asks, "Can you help me with this project?"
You respond:

"I'm learning to prioritize myself."

It's sincere and firm.

Phrase 76.

"I'm making space for what truly matters."

This phrase shows intentionality and clarity. It lets others know your no is part of a purposeful choice to focus on what aligns with your values and goals.

When to use it:

- When declining distractions or less important requests
- When setting priorities for personal or professional growth
- When you want to emphasize thoughtful decision-making

Example:

A friend invites you to an event that doesn't align with your goals.
You say:

"I'm making space for what truly matters."

It's focused and empowering.

Phrase 77.

"I'm choosing to protect my well-being."

This phrase communicates that your no is a form of self-care. It emphasizes the importance of looking after yourself and sets a clear, compassionate boundary.

When to use it:

- When declining invitations that may affect your mental or physical health
- When you need to enforce limits with friends or colleagues
- When reinforcing your commitment to self-care

Example:

A coworker asks, "Can you stay late to finish this report?"

You respond:

"I'm choosing to protect my well-being."

It's honest, respectful, and firm.

Phrase 78.

"I'm not able to take that on at this time."

This phrase is clear and polite, setting a firm boundary while acknowledging your current limitations. It communicates respect for both yourself and the requestor.

When to use it:

- When declining additional work or favours
- When you want to avoid overcommitting
- When maintaining professionalism while setting limits

Example:
A friend asks, "Can you help me move this weekend?"
You respond:

"I'm not able to take that on at this time."

It's straightforward and considerate.

79.

"I'm focusing on my priorities right now."

This phrase highlights your commitment to what matters most. It communicates a respectful but firm boundary, making it clear your "no" is intentional and purpose driven.

When to use it:

- When declining additional tasks that conflict with your goals
- When someone requests your time, but it doesn't align with your priorities
- When asserting control over your schedule

Example:

A colleague asks, "Can you attend this extra meeting?"

You respond:

"I'm focusing on my priorities right now."

It's clear, polite, and assertive.

Phrase 80.

"I'm setting limits to protect my peace."

This phrase expresses your intention to maintain inner calm and well-being. It helps others understand that your "no" is part of preserving your mental and emotional health.

When to use it:

- When declining emotionally taxing requests
- When needing to avoid burnout or overwhelm
- When communicating boundaries in personal or professional relationships

Example:

A friend asks, "Can you help me with a difficult issue?"

You respond:

"I'm setting limits to protect my peace."

It's respectful, honest, and firm.

Phrase 81.

"I have to focus on my own growth right now."

This phrase centre's your refusal on personal development and self-care. It sets a positive boundary that emphasizes your commitment to becoming the best version of yourself.

When to use it:

- When declining distractions or obligations that don't serve your growth
- When communicating priorities with friends or colleagues
- When establishing new personal boundaries

Example:
A friend invites you to a night out that conflicts with your goals.
You say:

"I have to focus on my own growth right now."

It's sincere, respectful, and empowering.

Phrase 82.

"I'm not able to give this the attention it deserves."

This phrase shows that you value quality and are unwilling to commit half-heartedly. It politely declines the request while maintaining respect for both parties.

When to use it:

- When you're overcommitted and want to avoid rushing
- When declining projects or favours that need full dedication
- When you want to be honest about your capacity

Example:
A colleague asks, "Can you lead this presentation?"
You respond:

"I'm not able to give this the attention it deserves."

It's clear, honest, and respectful.

Phrase 83.

"I'm choosing to say no to protect my mental health."

This phrase is a clear and honest boundary that prioritizes your emotional well-being. It helps others understand the importance of your refusal without inviting guilt or debate.

When to use it:

- When declining stressful requests or interactions
- When setting boundaries with people who don't understand your limits
- When emphasizing the importance of self-care

Example:

A coworker asks, "Can you take on this extra task?"

You respond:

"I'm choosing to say no to protect my mental health."

It's firm, compassionate, and self-respecting.

Phrase 84.

"I'm prioritizing my well-being right now."

This phrase highlights the importance of your health and balance. It communicates that your refusal is a necessary act of self-care.

When to use it:

- When declining social invitations that feel draining
- When setting limits to avoid burnout
- When reinforcing boundaries with friends, family, or coworkers

Example:

A friend asks, "Can you come out tonight?"

You respond:

"I'm prioritizing my well-being right now."

It's honest, respectful, and clear.

Phrase 85.

"That doesn't fit with my current plans."

This phrase communicates a clear boundary based on your priorities and schedule. It's respectful and direct, making your "no" easy to understand and accept.

When to use it:

- When declining invitations or requests that conflict with your agenda
- When setting limits around your time management
- When you want to maintain focus on your goals

Example:
A friend asks, "Can you join the weekend trip?"
You respond:

"That doesn't fit with my current plans."

It's straightforward and firm.

Phrase 86.

"I'm not able to take on more commitments right now."

This phrase communicates your current limitations clearly and respectfully. It helps others understand that your refusal isn't personal but a matter of capacity.

When to use it:

- When feeling overwhelmed by existing responsibilities
- When asked to join additional projects or favours
- When setting firm boundaries for your own well-being

Example:

A colleague asks, "Can you help with this new task?"

You respond:

"I'm not able to take on more commitments right now."

It's honest and clear.

Phrase 87.

"I'm focusing on what's most important to me."

This phrase centre's your refusal around your values and priorities. It communicates that your "no" is intentional and tied to what truly matters in your life.

When to use it:

- When declining distractions or unrelated requests
- When asserting boundaries to protect your goals
- When reinforcing your commitment to your own path

Example:

A friend invites you to a social event during your work hours.

You respond:

"I'm focusing on what's most important to me."

It's clear, respectful, and firm.

Phrase 88.

"That's outside of what I can commit to right now."

This phrase clearly communicates your current limits without negativity or excuses. It's respectful and straightforward, helping set firm boundaries.

When to use it:

- When asked to take on additional responsibilities you can't handle
- When you want to politely decline without over-explaining
- When maintaining your energy and focus is important

Example:

A colleague asks, "Can you join the new project team?"
You respond:

"That's outside of what I can commit to right now."

It's polite, firm, and clear.

Phrase 89.

"I'm saying no to honour my boundaries."

This phrase highlights your commitment to protecting yourself. It shows that your refusal is a positive, necessary act of self-respect.

When to use it:

- When others question your refusals
- When setting clear personal or professional limits
- When prioritizing your mental and emotional health

Example:

A friend pressures you to attend an event.

You respond:

"I'm saying no to honour my boundaries."

It's firm, clear, and empowering.

Phrase 90.

"I'm choosing peace over pressure."

This phrase communicates that you prioritize your mental and emotional well-being over external demands. It sets a clear boundary while emphasizing your choice for calm.

When to use it:

- When you feel overwhelmed by requests or expectations
- When declining invitations that cause stress
- When reinforcing the importance of your inner peace

Example:

A colleague asks you to work late again. You respond:

"I'm choosing peace over pressure."

It's calm, firm, and respectful.

Phrase 91.

"I'm focused on my priorities and need to say no."

This phrase makes your refusal about honouring your commitments. It's clear and respectful, helping others understand your boundaries.

When to use it:

- When declining distractions from your goals
- When reinforcing limits in work or personal life
- When you want to maintain focus without guilt

Example:
A friend invites you to join a new hobby group.
You respond:

"I'm focused on my priorities and need to say no."

It's assertive and straightforward.

Phrase 92.

"I'm protecting my time and energy."

This phrase emphasizes self-care and boundary-setting. It clearly communicates that your refusal comes from a place of self-respect.

When to use it:

- When you want to avoid overextending yourself
- When declining requests that drain your energy
- When reinforcing your limits with others

Example:

A coworker asks, "Can you help with this last-minute task?"

You respond:

"I'm protecting my time and energy."

It's honest, clear, and firm.

Phrase 93.

"I'm focusing on what matters most to me."

This phrase communicates your intention to prioritize the most important things in your life. It helps others understand why you must say no without inviting guilt.

When to use it:

- When declining invitations or requests that don't align with your goals
- When reinforcing boundaries around your time
- When emphasizing your personal priorities

Example:

A friend invites you to a party during a busy work week.

You respond:

"I'm focusing on what matters most to me."

It's clear, respectful, and assertive.

Phrase 94.

"I'm choosing to say no to protect my peace of mind."

This phrase clearly states that your refusal is an act of self-care. It emphasizes the importance of mental and emotional well-being and sets a firm boundary.

When to use it:

- When declining requests that cause stress or anxiety
- When setting limits with people who don't respect your boundaries
- When prioritizing your own calm and stability

Example:

A friend asks, "Can you help me with this stressful situation?"

You respond:

"I'm choosing to say no to protect my peace of mind."

It's firm, clear, and nurturing.

Phrase 95.

"I'm taking time to focus on my well-being."

This phrase communicates that your refusal is rooted in self-care and prioritizing your health. It helps others understand your boundaries with compassion.

When to use it:

- When declining invitations or favours that might drain you
- When setting limits with friends or family
- When emphasizing the importance of self-care

Example:
A friend invites you to a late-night gathering.
You respond:

"I'm taking time to focus on my well-being."

It's honest, respectful, and firm.

Phrase 96.

"I'm focusing on my own journey right now."

This phrase communicates that your refusal stems from prioritizing your personal growth and path. It gently reminds others that you are committed to your own development and that some requests don't align with where you are.

When to use it:

- When turning down social invitations that distract from your goals
- When declining commitments that pull you away from your focus
- When reinforcing your dedication to self-improvement

Example:
A friend asks, "Want to join the weekend trip?"
You respond:

"I'm focusing on my own journey right now."

It's clear, respectful, and focused.

Phrase 97.

"I'm learning that my 'no' is a gift I give to myself and others."

This phrase transforms the act of saying no into an empowering, loving choice. It reminds both you and others that setting boundaries nurtures your well-being and respects the quality of your commitments.

When to use it:

- When gently explaining your refusal to close ones
- When reinforcing healthy boundaries with kindness
- When embracing self-love as part of your journey

Example:

A friend asks, "Can you help me with this favour?"

You respond:

"I'm learning that my 'no' is a gift I give to myself and others."

It's graceful, heartfelt, and empowering.

Phrase 98.

"I'm choosing what nourishes my soul and letting go of what doesn't."

This phrase beautifully conveys that your refusal is a mindful act of self-care and emotional nourishment. It emphasizes the importance of surrounding yourself with positivity and protecting your inner peace.

When to use it:

- When declining activities or requests that drain you
- When setting boundaries in relationships
- When prioritizing your emotional and spiritual health

Example:
A friend asks, "Can you attend the weekend gathering?"
You respond:

"I'm choosing what nourishes my soul and letting go of what doesn't."

It's elegant, intentional, and deeply respectful.

Phrase 99.

"I honour my needs by saying no when I must."

This phrase communicates deep self-respect and accountability. It acknowledges that saying no is a vital part of honouring yourself and maintaining your well-being.

When to use it:

- When setting firm boundaries with loved ones or colleagues
- When you want to affirm your commitment to self-care
- When refusing requests that compromise your needs

Example:

A family member asks, "Can you help me this weekend?"

You respond:

"I honour my needs by saying no when I must."

It's respectful, clear, and powerful.

Phrase 100.

"My peace is more important than pleasing others."

This phrase is a bold declaration that puts your well-being first. It reminds you and others that your happiness and calm are valid priorities — even if it means saying no.

When to use it:

- When pressured to say yes out of obligation or guilt
- When setting firm boundaries for your mental health
- When reinforcing your right to self-care

Example:

Someone insists, "Just say yes this one time."

You respond:

"My peace is more important than pleasing others."

It's courageous, clear, and empowering.

Closing Page: Your Journey to Saying No Without Guilt

Congratulations on completing this book!

You've built a toolkit of powerful, respectful ways to say no — without guilt, apology, or regret.

Remember:

Saying no is not selfish.

It's the most important form of self-respect.

Every time you say no, you are saying yes — to your peace, your priorities, and your well-being.

Certificate of Completion

This certifies that

_____

has successfully completed
100 Ways to Say No Without Guilt
and committed to honouring their
boundaries with confidence,
kindness, and self-respect.

Signed, with courage and integrity,

Signed:

_____

Date:

_____

Final Words

Thank you for purchasing this journal, I hope it helped you as much as I intended it to. If you enjoyed this journal, there are a few more books you can purchase on my Amazon Seller page like this.

The Identity I Chose: The Most Neglected Person Is Yourself - Isaac Ajala

Don't Leave It Till Later: The Procrastination Journal – Shatter Procrastination Cycles and Forge Unstoppable, Discipline-Driven Habits

The Chosen Identity Journal: A Journal To Becoming Whoever You Want To Be. – Isaac Ajala

At the time of reading this, some books may not be out because they are not finished/completed yet. So, to find updates on the books, follow my TikTok page at:

https://www.tiktok.com/@imisaacajala

FOR MORE BOOKS BY ME!

Printed in Dunstable, United Kingdom

64885626R00122